For Peter

With thanks to Sally and Andy Barr at East Lenham Farm and to Peter Lamb in Broadchalke.

Text and illustration © Susan Steggall 2014

First published in Great Britain and the USA in 2014 by
Frances Lincoln Children's Books
74-77 White Lion Street
London, N1 9PF

A CIP catalogue record for this book is available from the British Library.

ISBN: 978-1-84780-489-1

Printed in China

1 3 5 7 9 8 6 4 2

Following the Tractor

Susan Steggall

F

FRANCES LINCOLN
CHILDREN'S BOOKS

The winter soil is sleeping,
when the tractor comes along,
pulling its plough through
the cold, hard ground.

And the birds fly down,
to see what can be found,
by following the tractor
around and around.

Then the tractor brings a seed drill,
to sow the soil with seeds,

and the birds fly down,
to see what can be found.

And the tractor brings a spreader,
to fertilise the fields.

And the rain comes down, down and down.
The farmer's old car gets stuck in the mud.

And still the rain comes down.

But then, the sun comes out,
and the seeds come up.

And they grow, **and they grow, and they grow.**

Until the summer soil is scorching
when the harvester comes,
rattling its reels across the hot, hard ground.

And the birds fly down,
to see what can be found,
by following the harvester around and around.

Then a big truck comes,
to carry the grain to the mill,

the tractor brings a baler,
to bale up the straw on the hill,

and the tractor brings a trailer,

to carry the straw to the farm.

But when the winter brings a chill,

the tractor's safe inside the barn.

So, the tractor, it is sleeping
when the farmer comes along,
lugging his load across the cold, hard ground.

And the cows come down,
to see what can be found,
by following the farmer around and around.